T0368443

MASTER THE MOMENT, INC.
CONNI BLANCHARD, PRESIDENT

THINK

—— AND ——

GROW
THIN!

**YOUR SHORTCUT TO HOW I DROPPED
AND KEPT OFF 10 SIZES.**

Secrets to
Mastering Your
Self-esteem,
Self-reliance,
and
Self-talk!

CONNI BLANCHARD

Balboa Press books may be ordered through booksellers or by contacting:

Balboa Press
A Division of Hay House
1663 Liberty Drive
Bloomington, IN 47403
www.balboapress.com
844-682-1282

Interior Image Credit: Ruth Ganev, Portrait Photographer, ruth@ruthganev.com

ISBN: 979-8-7652-2800-5 (sc)
ISBN: 979-8-7652-2801-2 (e)

Library of Congress Control Number: 2022907850

Print information available on the last page.

Balboa Press rev. date: 04/26/2022

DEDICATION

This is dedicated to my mom who shared this valuable life lesson with me as a teenager when my hormones first started raging: There will always be someone greater and lesser in the world at everything you choose to do, so only compare yourself to you!

Think, Act and Conduct Yourself Like The Person you Intend To Become.

- John C. Maxwell

https://linktr.ee/MastertheMomentInc

CONTENTS

M: MASTER Self-Esteem: Learn to raise your standards as you learn that you cannot outperform your self-image. You have dignity as a miraculous human being. Your body is a machine and it will respond when you make better choices.

T: THE Imagination and Self-Reliance: You are your own best coach, you know yourself intimately better than anyone else knows you. Learn to teach your body ahead of time what your compelling future will feel like. Practice living in a state of grace, reach for the feelings of what it would be like to feel healthy and abundant to draw those states of being into your life!

I was a deeply emotional eater who rewarded and punished myself with food for decades. I have transformed my mind and body by learning to master the moment. I have retrained my thinking to focus on my choices in 5-minute windows, 24 hours at a time. As I learned to retrain my thoughts, behaviors, and habits my body has transformed from my worst enemy into my very best friend. As I develop the courage to step onto the global stage to share my message, my mission is to be an authentic mentor for emotional eaters everywhere and a catalyst for real change! My message is powerful and it is real. I must share the important news that there is an alternative to deprivation dieting, excessive exercise, and nonsense. I am sharing my authentic life experience to restore self-worth, a sense of dignity, and hope for women who suffer from poor self-esteem, no self-reliance and debilitating self-talk. Starting 40 years ago, my only crutch for my emotions was eating. My body grew to be bigger than ever, for me, and I felt awkward because my outside appearance was so far off how I felt inside. My self-esteem had plummeted. I was desperate to find a way to stop hating the way I looked in the mirror since I felt uncomfortable all day every day. For years, every morning I used to criticize myself and I punished and rewarded myself with food throughout my day. Each night I fell into bed feeling worse than when I woke up which was a vicious, painful cycle. I knew that I had to work on my self-esteem, for starters. I tapped into my powerful imagination and I learned self-reliance the hard way. There was no internet to seek out support when I started my journey. I loved the insights in the book *Think and Grow Rich* by Napoleon Hill. In 1937, the book came out and he never renewed the copyright license. This is my true story of how I adapted the concepts of his book of valuable lessons to my own personal journey of inner transformation from an overweight teenager obsessed with food and with pleasing my parents to dropping and keeping off 10 sizes, living with renewed energy and hope for my future. Over time, I structured my steps to success into my MTM methodology for you to follow in order because they are cumulative, which is exciting! Your starting point is to grasp that your brain is a record of your past. Your life experiences, thoughts, behaviors, and habits got you to this moment. The secret for you to succeed on a different plan back to your true self requires you to pay attention to your choices. You must give yourself permission to reach for a better feeling thought. Allow yourself to lean into your compelling future rather than dwelling on the past. Sometimes you have to hit rock bottom before you make a change but sometimes you can just decide that enough is enough and you understand that you deserve to feel better now! Rewiring your brain by retraining your thoughts and habits is possible by following my MTM Methodology. My hope is that you will develop courage to use these free tools to stop suffering in silence for eating all of your emotions. You cannot outperform your self-image so that is where your journey begins It is possible and exciting to re-channel your intensity towards food. Please know that you are not stuck! This moment is all you have and all you will ever need to change your future! Give yourself permission to tap into your powerful imagination as you learn to think differently!

To Your Success!

Conni Blanchard, Master The Moment, Inc, president

Master The Moment.Inc

CONNI BLANCHARD, PRESIDENT

HOW TO: THINK AND GROW THIN!

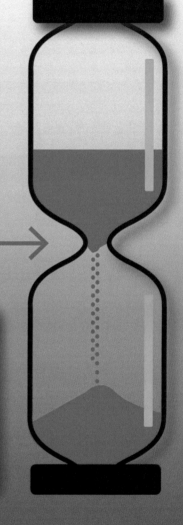

MASTER
YOUR SELF-ESTEEM

THE
IMAGINATION + SELF-RELIANCE

MOMENT
SELF-TALK IN THE NOW

| FOCUS ON YOUR FUTURE | + | ACT LIKE WHO YOU INTEND TO BECOME | + | REACH FOR A BETTER FEELING THOUGHT |

M: MASTER Self-Esteem: Learn to raise your standards as you learn that you cannot outperform your self-image. You have dignity as a miraculous human being. Your body is a machine and it will respond when you make better choices.

- You can never outperform your own self-image. – Maxwell Maltz
- We think in secret and it comes to pass. Environment is but our looking glass. – James Allen
- Whatever your mind can conceive and believe, it can achieve! A Burning Desire to be and to do is the starting point from which we dreamers must take off. Dreams are not born of indifference, laziness, or lack of ambition. – Napoleon Hill
- It's time to be defined by a vision of your future instead of by the memories of your past -Dr. Joe Dispenza

If you want to go from self-defeated to self-driven and you are ready for these secrets, you already possess what it takes to get started on your inner transformation. The rest of the knowledge, skills, and tools will become more real for you as the concepts reach your mind. Your outer transformation is the by-product or the result of improving the way you think and feel about yourself, deep in your heart and mind. Your thoughts are powerful things. Life is strange since both your successes and your failures have their roots in simple experiences. Your brain is a record of the past. It got you to exactly where you are today. As you take time to appreciate yourself for a moment and realize that you are a miraculous machine, you can begin to develop an appreciation of your body as a miraculous set of cooperative internal systems. A clear image of your ideal self is all you need to achieve success. The steps of my MTM methodology begin with improving the image you have of your best body, in your mind. When your learn to master the moment, in 5-minute windows, 24 hours at a time, your self-esteem can be restored so quickly that you'll wonder how you went all those years being your worst enemy! When you begin to think and grow thin, you will observe that thinness, which is simply what I mean by feeling at ease in your own body, begins with a state of mind, with a definiteness of purpose. I spent over thirty-five years developing and analyzing my own transformation. I am sharing the principles that made the most impact on my success as you begin your journey so that you will not have to struggle as hard as I did for decades to identify and repeat what worked and disregarded what didn't work. Your thoughts, behaviors, and actions got you to where you are today. If you believe in your limitations you will stay stuck. Instead, you must stay focused on learning to think differently until you succeed. Determination is a critical component. You really have to want it, deep down! If you have never taken time to apply these principles then you owe it to yourself to start to try now. The exciting fact is that you do have the power to control your thoughts! The universe is pure energy! All around us is a form of universal power that adapts itself to the energy of the thoughts you hold in your mind and influences you to transmute your thoughts into things. This power does not discriminate between self-debilitating thoughts and constructive thoughts so your thoughts will make you feel worse just as quickly as your better thoughts will influence you to act upon thoughts of your own dignity and self-worth. Your brain becomes magnetic with the dominating thoughts you hold in your mind. Before you can accumulate self-love in abundance, you must magnetize your mind with the intense desire for self-worth. You must become conscious of what your ideal body size is for you until the desire to look and feel your best drives you to create definite plans for acquiring it. Maintain a spirit of open-mindedness as you read about my methodology that developed over three decades of my life experience as a deeply emotional eater. Take time to absorb these ideas so that you too can restore faith in your ability to think less self-defeating thoughts. My hope is that you also learn to re-channel your intensity towards food to get you where you want to be, without deprivation, intermittent fasting, extreme exercising or anything absurd that would never last over time anyway!

- The instant you accept responsibility for everything in your life is the moment you acquire the power to change it. -Ed Mylett
- Your struggle is your strength. If you can resist becoming negative, bitter, or hopeless, in time, your struggles will give you everything. -Bryant Gill
- If you are not willing to learn, no one can help you. If you are determined to learn, no one can stop you. -Zig Ziglar

DESIRE
MY STORY

From seat 2A, out my window, the Rockies were more magnificent than I ever imagined. My stomach was in knots! As the plane descended over the Rocky Mountains, all at once, I somehow switched my focus from the guilt and burden of my past to the bright possibilities of my future as the plane glided onto the runway. I arrived with high hopes for myself at CU, Boulder in the fall of 1982. I went inside my mind, I felt the limiting beliefs and guilt that I carried as I graduated from my small high school on the east coast, lifted all at once! I experienced the lightbulb moment of actively switching my thinking from dwelling on the guilt of my past behaviors to focusing on my compelling future! It was such an extremely hopeful feeling! It opened my eyes to the rest of the world and I thought the sky is the limit! As I made my way down the airport terminal in Denver, Colorado with my large suitcase and larger thighs making noise as I waddled quickly along, I decided that right then I was going to use this new environment to get thin! This desire to be comfortable in my body became my one consuming obsession. It was my one burning desire to become who I was supposed to be, a lean and strong woman without the burden and self-torment of being an emotional eater. It was not a hope! It was not a wish! It was a keen pulsating desire, which transcended everything else. I replaced my self-hatred and debilitating self-talk with a deep fury inside my head and redirected it towards really wanting to feel better. I did not understand at the time, but my ability to refocus on my goal instead of on the past was the beginning of my journey out of the self-inflicted misery of my situation. I was always muscular and I learned years ago that muscle weighs more than fat. For that reason, I never focused solely on the scale but instead on my deep desire to be the person I knew I could be when I looked into the full-length mirror. Over time, I felt this desire to my core. I let this desire burn inside me 24/7. Over time, the desire to have my outside match my inside guided my days and long nights through college. As I write this, 40 years later, I am still an emotional eater but I retrained my thinking and I am down 10 sizes. I look back now and I see that my intense and dominating dream of my life had become a reality. I truly believe that your desire to want to improve from deep in your gut is the critical first step. I absolutely got inside my head and that is the point. I am here to help you get inside your own head to initiate your inner transformation! Retraining your thinking is free and it is your vital first step, to desire to transform back to your true self. There are so many choices on which How to program to follow. Each has their benefits so one of them will work for you but only if you get your head straight first. You cannot outperform your self-image. I am sharing my journey for you to learn the steps to take to get your head straight so that you may succeed instead of verbally abusing yourself for always choosing too much food to feel better as you celebrate or punish yourself with food to cope with everything you are going through at this time in your life. Until you go inside your head and your heart and decide that your time is now to redirect your intense emotional connection to food, you cannot truly evolve into your best body. My point is that there is no feeling of deprivation when you focus on your desire to be your best self. Life is short. It is not too late, your body is a machine and it will respond to how you treat it. Micro-progress is progress. As you learn to tap into that deep desire to look and feel better, you can actively train your mind to let go of the baggage of the past and the fear of the future. You can teach yourself to stay present, to control your choices in 5-minute windows, 24 hours at a time. Honestly, that's all you have, the very next moment, and the best part of this deeply personal journey is that's all you need to do - simply reach for a better feeling thought than you have right now, over and over and over! You deserve to hear the truth. You are truly capable of desiring improvement so much that you can change your thoughts about yourself and the story you tell yourself about yourself when you are by yourself. I agree with Tom Bilyeu who states that this is the most important conversation you will ever have in life. I practiced gradually improving my story over three decades so I was able to change my entire body from the inside out. You need to know that it is possible to retrain your mind to believe in your ability to desire progress. You can increase your level of desire from self-hatred, to blah, to well, maybe…,to a firm conviction that YES, you do desire to progress more than you want to keep up the self-sabotage. Your progress and getting thin which is truly a relative term is as real for you as you tell yourself it is! Now I am at my own most comfortable size, defined by me, which is the critical part for you to grasp, your ideal for you can only come from you as an emotional eater, the struggle is real. You are not alone. I have to use self-talk and consistently prioritize my desire for micro-progress every single 24 hours. Desire for your own micro-progress can become your inner thought process for the rest of your life. You must make a committed decision to change your focus from the habit of feeling bad about your thoughts, behaviors, and habits of yesterday and stay riveted on your future. Dr. Joe Dispenza, neuroscientist, teaches us that we have the power to become almost supernatural. What this means is that as an emotional eater you can teach your mind what to think instead of reactively plodding through a busy day as I did, from a morning doughnut to an evening third helping of food, eating past the point when your stomach hurts from being full. This new way to think is truly empowering! The desire you have inside to feel better must grow. Practice leaning into your compelling vision you have of yourself. Reprioritize your desire to take in excess food with the desire to imagine the feeling of what it feels like as your ideal size. It is doable! Dr. Joe's message is valid for us emotional eaters. Simply practice teaching your body emotionally what your best body feels like ahead of time. This is wonderful news! There is no such thing as stopping being an emotional eater when every thought, every 24 hours is about food. This took me over three decades of practice and I am telling my story as proof that your mind is your best weapon! No one talks about the deliberate focus required to lean into the feeling of already being your ideal size. Without changing the way you see yourself in your mind, you cannot ever progress. Your focus must become an obsession, to tap into feeling of what it is like to be your ideal size. Dwelling on the extreme discomfort of how you feel right now will never ever get you to your goal without suffering! I have struggled with this truth and I know first-hand that desire is the starting point required on your journey. Your body is your very best friend. You may just not know it yet! You can learn how to re-channel your intensity towards eating and use that intensity towards empowering yourself to make the best next choice in the next 5-minute window, 24 hours at a time. As you continue to improve the choices you make, your heavy burden of your guilt will begin to go away. You will feel lighter, less bogged down by your past thoughts, behaviors, and habits. You can learn to think differently and act differently as you talk to yourself more correctly. Imagine being excited for the new day and going to bed feeling better than when you woke up instead of worse. It is possible! Desire is your first critical step. You must really crave change to the point of innate desire to get good at acting like the person you intend to become! You already have what it takes to get back your self–esteem, your self-reliance, and improved self-talk. You must deeply desire to develop those traits in yourself. Beating yourself up for eating too much and not having the self-discipline to control your behaviors when it comes to eating can be self-debilitating and very painful. You already have what it takes to flip those conversations on their head! Your body is a machine. Your body functions the way it is supposed to function, meaning it will respond to exactly how you treat it! The amazing part is that your body does respond to improved habits, even at a cellular level. This means that if you eat one less potato chip tomorrow than you normally would take in, your body has to respond with less elevated sodium in your system! Yes, progress begins as micro-progress. You must first desire deep down improvement. If it does not bother you to be horribly uncomfortable in your skin 10, 20, even 30 years from now, if this is acceptable, then put this down and go back to your state of mediocrity. I am here to tell you that if your desire burns inside of you, out of spite for your past, or in spite of your past, you are in for a treat! You can work hard to retrain your thinking and one day, sooner than it took me, which was decades, you will feel excited for your future! Most emotional eaters become discouraged about their uncontrolled eating, simply become more and more uncomfortable and then eventually give up on themselves. Your body is a machine, so it will not and cannot give up on you even if you want to give up on it! Desire is your fuel to retrain yourself in so many ways. Portion control is the very first step. A strong desire to attempt to focus on portion control, ahead of time is the very best start on your journey back to loving yourself and to your ideal size. You can also lean into the feeling of desire to feel better than you did 24 hours ago. You get to work on your muscle maturity as it evolves as well. Light resistance weight training is a habit that your body requires to transform outwardly. I encourage you to make a point to dream while you are awake! Desire to be your true self and wanting to sustain your ideal body size takes ambitious thinking! You have the tools inside your own mind. You do not need a coach, a program, or a rigid plan to get started. You simply need to promise to continue to desire to improve upon your story! This is not a How-To Diet or Exercise Plan or magic pill. This was written to help you get your head straight to increase your self-esteem, your self-reliance, and your self-talk. Pre-keto, pre-weight watchers, pre-Noom, pre-Vshred, pre-whatever plan you can think of – once you learn you are capable of improving on a cellular level, you may finally succeed the next time you try the plan of your choice! You can then finally stop the painful, debilitating feelings that you project into your head, simply for being an emotional eater.

- Our only limitations are the ones we set up in our own mind. –Napoleon Hill
- All personal breakthroughs begin with a change in beliefs. – Tony Robbins

DESIRE
NAPOLEON HILL'S STRATEGY
APPLIED TO EMOTIONAL EATING

The method of transforming your mental image of your ideal body into its physical equivalent consists of six practical actions.

1. Fix in your mind your exact size that you desire. It is not sufficient merely to say, I want to be smaller. Be definite as to the size. There is a psychological reason for being specific.

2. Determine exactly what you intend to give back to your family, spouse, or to your community as you show up as your heartfelt self. There is no such reality as something for nothing. Sharing your new thoughts about your new way to think about yourself is enough, if you vocalize it along your journey, you can regain your self-esteem.

3. Establish a definite date when you intend to reach your goal or the definite date you will start feeling momentum, whichever makes more sense for you.

4. Create a definite plan for carrying out your desire, and begin at once, whether you are ready or not, to put this plan into action.

5. Write out a clear concise statement of the size you intend to work towards, name the time limit for its acquisition, state what you will give back along the way, and describe clearly the plan through which you intend to reach it. You could share your plan with a loved one as a reinforcement of your plan to make this journey real for you.

6. Read your statement aloud, twice daily, once just before bed and once after waking up, as you read it, do see, feel and believe yourself already at your ideal size.

You may complain that it is impossible for you to see yourself at your ideal size before you actually reach it. If you truly desire to be comfortable in your skin so much that your desire is an obsession it will be easier to convince yourself that you will acquire it. These instructions may appear impractical. It may be helpful to know that I dropped and kept off over 10 sizes and at age 57, I continue to improve daily using these six action steps. You've really got to want it!

- Life is one big tug of war between mediocrity and trying to find your best self. -David Goggins
- Stand guard at the door of your mind. -Jim Rohn
- Believe you can and you're halfway there. –Theodore Roosevelt

FAITH
MY STORY

Holding my breath, stepping onto the cold bathroom floor before my morning shower, hoping this would be the day that the digital scale went down a couple of tenths instead of steadily up. I used to dread the first part of each new morning. I lost faith in my ability to feel any self- worth in my late teens. It was maddening! I knew I was a self-proclaimed emotional eater since I celebrated every small win, an A on a test or a great homework assignment done, with dessert. I punished myself if I fell behind in class or missed a question on a test by overeating way past the point of being full. I found no other way to comfort myself other than eating, I was a loner...I had peers who were friendly classmates, but on a typical Friday night, I preferred to bury myself in books with a large bowl of microwave popcorn smothered in butter to talking on the phone or to going out. In the age before the internet, my thoughts were all I had to keep me company. Decades later, my imagination would become my secret advantage but at the time, it was very lonely. I was a bookworm and I used to beat myself up verbally. My self-destructive habits and behaviors led to binge eating and feeling worse for it afterwards. I bullied myself and no one ever spoke to me so horribly as how I talked to myself from the moment that I woke up for hating how I felt until my midnight trip to the fridge for my third full dinner, while my family was sound asleep. I learned self-talk but it was deeply negative! I felt guilty and very heavy regardless of my academic or sports achievements. Yes, I was actually on the track team, but my slap in the face came in my senior year, during spring training.

I pulled on my tight polyester uniform pants and waddled self-consciously from the locker room to the track. Inside my head I was trying not to acknowledge the deep feeling of disconnect between my thunderous thighs and the person I was inside my heart. I had eaten my emotions for the entire school year. My track coach pulled me aside, and said, Conni, I know you like running the two mile, but this season, why don't you bow out and just throw the shot put for us... I had never felt so mortified, but of course, I went along with the plan. My uniform pants made noise as my thighs rubbed together as I walked, carrying a shot put to practice, it was deeply embarrassing to my core. For that reason, I spent the last season of high school in shame. It was painful on my knees and in my heart because of how distended and uncomfortable I was in my body. My consequences were a direct result of the way I talked to myself. I clearly remember lying in bed at night, trying to think of the worst possible adjectives to use against myself for having no self-discipline around food. This degrading experience led to a pivotal moment on my ride home one evening after a long humiliating practice of throwing the shot and stretching out. I pondered for a moment, if I stop being so mean to myself and I could trust the process of the results as I made better choices would my self-esteem improve? I had no choice but to latch onto faith in my ability to improve, even if it was only micro-progress. Faith in my ability to think better thoughts was a brand new idea to me. I was so swollen full of excess calories that I truly doubted my body's ability to deflate my fat cells. It was so deeply painful to continue to talk myself down 24/7 that instead I chose to re-channel my intensity towards food and my self-esteem began to improve. Self-esteem is an inner experience not an outer thing that is dependent on anyone else's opinion of you. In your core, you know whether your self-esteem needs improvement. I decided to pour myself into books about Physiology to learn how the body works and how our fat cells can get swollen and deflated, but never go away. I imagined my cells as swollen grapes and was truly fascinated with the possibility that I could possibly deflate as I made better choices.

It was a long road since the internet did not exist yet so I had no access to resources that you have at your fingertips now. I remember that I had to stop using the scale as my tool for a while and have faith in my micro-progress. I used the way my clothes fit to reinforce my faith in my ability to select words less than debilitating self-hatred. It took decades of reinforcing deep faith in my body as a miraculous machine to get down 10 sizes. Having faith in your ability to make better choices means that improvement is as possible for you as it was for me and in less time! It is difficult to retrain your thinking and to keep the faith especially if it is a brand new habit to not dwell on how much you hate how you look and feel right now. Your body cannot not respond to exactly what you choose to take in next and that is an exciting fact. As you develop faith in your body's ability to respond to your choices, you will be on your way to becoming your best self. Stopping being an emotional eater makes no sense! It how some of us are wire and it is your superpower! Your body will respond to changes that you make only as quickly as you choose to treat yourself more kindly, with dignity and respect. Your results will astound you! I curated and followed my methodology for you to follow to stop suffering by learning to master the moment, in 5-minute windows, 24 hours at a time. Yours is a deeply personal journey. You know your current level of self-debilitating phrases and thoughts. Reach for those thoughts, isolate each one, and replace it with a little tiny bit better phrase and action. I am not selling you a diet plan or telling you how to lose weight overnight. This is my very real, very personal journey of transformation over three decades. Starting right now, you get to give yourself permission to cherish the next moment knowing it is yours to make a bit of a better choice than you did yesterday, or even one hour ago. No one talks about the faith in yourself that is required to gather momentum on your way to your ideal size. Plateaus are real and they can be discouraging. Debilitating self-talk about how you feel right now will never ever get you to your goal without suffering! Your body truly is your very best friend you may just not know it yet. Your unique body is yours, what a glorious gift you have been given! You deserve to respect yourself even as you feel no self-control around food. Your burden can be lifted and your journey of faith in yourself, towards true self-esteem starts right now!

- Just for the record darling, not all positive change feels positive in the beginning. –S.C. Lourie
- Don't be pushed around by the fears in your mind. Be led by the dreams in your heart. –Roy T. Bennett
- What you think about expands, so be careful to guard the door of your mind. –Dr. Wayne Dyer

FAITH
NAPOLEON HILL'S STRATEGY APPLIED TO EMOTIONAL EATING

Visualization and belief in the attainment of your goal is critical. Faith is the head chemist of the mind. When faith is blended with the vibration of thought your subconscious mind instantly picks up the vibration, translates it into its spiritual equivalent, and transmits it to Infinite Intelligence, as in the case of prayer. The emotions of faith and love are powerful positive emotions that can impact the vibration of thought that instantly reaches the subconscious mind, where it is changed into its spiritual equivalent, the only form that induces a response from Infinite Intelligence. Love and faith are psychic, related to the spiritual side of humanity. Faith is a state of mind that you can develop. Repetition or affirmation of orders to your subconscious mind is the only method of development of the emotion of faith in yourself. Your belief or faith is exactly what determines the action of your subconscious mind. Do be sure to get thoughts into your subconscious as if you were already in possession of what you are demanding, your ideal size body. By trying to maintain a positive mental attitude, it will be easier to reach the state of mind of faith to accept ideas and act upon them immediately.

- We all make mistakes, have struggles, and even regret things in our past. But you are not your mistakes, you are not your struggles, and you are here now with the power to shape your day and your future. -Steve Maraboli
- Rather than give up or be discouraged, if we keep a positive outlook we will find solutions to our issues will come much more easily. -Catherine Pulsifer

AUTOSUGGESTION
MY STORY

Another late weekend night, trying to fall asleep, painfully full from overeating, seeking out hurtful words to beat myself up for eating too much throughout the day. It was extremely painful to absorb that level of self-hatred down to my core. It was the most destructive use of autosuggestion. I was able to do this in the most powerful way, for several years. It was a very painful time in my entire life as an introvert who ate all of my emotions. I was so good at getting negative thoughts into my subconscious that I talked myself into a very negative spiral. My self-image spiraled downward throughout the end of high school. I told myself over time that because I could not control my emotions or limits at the dinner table, I was a horrible person. I talked myself into believing that I was socially inept and awkward with my peers because I was so heavy. I went to bed reaching for worse and worse words to make myself feel as bad as possible every night. I absorbed these debilitating ideas into my subconscious. These thoughts and feelings made me eat more the next day and feel worse about myself by the time I went to bed the next night. I was so strong mentally that I truly worked myself into a negative spiral. Every morning, waddling off to the bus, placing my bag lunch into my locker to eat in between classes, I admired the skinny girls and the cheerleaders, and I used autosuggestion to create feelings of inadequacy stronger than they ever truly were in reality. I was in advanced classes and I did not look ugly. I simply used autosuggestion to convince myself that I was unable to socialize with the slim girls so I forced myself to feel even more awkward than I was in our very small high school. Autosuggestion is what I mastered, in the most negative way imaginable. Nature has wired human beings so that we truly have absolute control over what ideas reach our subconscious. This pattern was so self-destructive that I continued to gain weight and lose my self-esteem. Autosuggestion was successful for me because I linked such negative emotions with my self-talk that reached my subconscious. This continued until I got into college. A huge campus across the country gave me a glimpse of what it would be like to feel better than self-loathing for being one of the biggest girls in my graduating class, 40 years ago. I had the faintest idea deep down that I could start over in a new much larger crowd. My self-talk gradually became a bit less destructive. At night, I was able to stop reaching for the absolute worst possible words and feelings about myself to end up waking up feeling worse than yesterday. I started using autosuggestion without realizing it to go into a neutral, self-accepting state of mind. I stopped crucifying myself over my poor choices I made when it came time to eat, which was all the time! It was very slow but the more I looked forward to a new environment across the country, I felt less bad about myself in the tiniest increments at first. Over time, as the summer progressed and I was getting ready for college, without even realizing it, I was autosuggesting thoughts and words differently, I felt less burdened at my core. I used this new habit to get out of very real self-hatred. I was still awkward in social situations because I told myself that I eat too much all the time so I was not worthy of listening to, and I was deep down, so far from my ideal size. It felt less burdensome to plod along and it was momentum and my self-talk that improved to get me where

I am today. I travelled across the country in August of 1982, and I shifted the emotions that I put into my self-talk. It was the beginning of the rest of my life. I am convinced that as I poured the feelings of hope and faith into my subconscious using autosuggestion it lightened the burden of self-hatred I had for myself just for being an emotional eater. I was able to evolve in my first few years in school by talking to myself more correctly. I was still heavy but as I transplanted new feelings and new better thoughts into my subconscious, I was able to absorb this new way of being. Fast forward four decades, and I am down 10 sizes and I play games with autosuggestion successfully to continue to improve my body. I cannot imagine saying anything negative about my body. I know deep in my core that my body is my best friend. I tell myself that my body is waiting for me to make my next choice. My body will respond to my next choice in direct proportion to what I take in and that fact is now truly fascinating. Autosuggestion has become a fun mental exercise. I make a point to practice reaching for a better feeling thought in 5-minute windows, 24 hours at a time. Autosuggestion is a mind trip! The truth is that it is actually empowering to have a strong emotional connection to food. It is your secret weapon, not your biggest weakness! The uncertainty and inner turmoil of the global pandemic we lived through is emotional fuel you can flip on its head, to drive your mind and body into a better state. You can re-channel the nervousness and stress with personal affirmations. It can be discouraging as you start out since it is a challenge to control and direct your emotions when you first try to do so. Your ability to use autosuggestion will depend on your ability to concentrate in 5-minute windows until you can obsess on specifically what you have in mind for your ideal body. Self-talk and letting thoughts get into your subconscious seems to be the most powerful for me late at night. As you lie in bed, with faith, talking to yourself, imagining already being in your ideal body. Repeating the affirmations that mean the most to you is a deeply personal experience. Only you know which thoughts you need to replace with better thoughts about your own body. You can get to the point where you feed empowering thoughts into your subconscious both morning and night. It takes time and practice to go from self-loathing to neutral to self-acceptance to hope and then to belief in yourself! It is doable. Pre-keto, pre-Noom, pre-weight watchers, it is critical that you begin to think better about your body. Autosuggestion is a uniquely personal tool and it is free! You are a miraculous machine and learning the power of autosuggestion makes it possible to be a role model again, for yourself, and for those who count on you!

- When you change the way you look at things, the things you look at change. -Dr. Wayne Dyer
- All personal breakthroughs begin with a change in beliefs. - Tony Robbins
- Take chances, make mistakes. That's how you grow. Pain nourishes your courage. You have to fail in order to practice being brave. -Mary Tyler Moore

AUTOSUGGESTION
NAPOLEON HILL'S STRATEGY
APPLIED TO EMOTIONAL EATING

The dominating thoughts that you permit to remain in your conscious mind will reach and influence your subconscious mind through the law of autosuggestion. Whether your thoughts are negative or positive this is true so this is why you must actively improve your thoughts. You have absolute control over the thoughts that reach your subconscious mind through your five senses. You may not always exercise that control so you may feel ashamed of your lack of self-control over food at a subconscious level. Through repetition your subconscious mind recognizes and acts only upon thoughts that were well mixed with emotion or feeling. Plain, unemotional words do not influence your mind. The ability to reach and influence your subconscious mind has its price. The price of the ability to influence your subconscious mind is persistence. You start by consistently trying to reach for a better feeling thought. Wisdom and cleverness alone will not attract and retain your goal. Using autosuggestion well will depend on how well you can concentrate upon a given desire until that desire becomes a burning obsession. It is critical to give yourself permission to feel and see yourself at your ideal body size in your mind. Consider the possibility of playing a perfectly legitimate trick on your subconscious mind by making it believe that the body you are visualizing is already yours. By autosuggestion, your subconscious mind must hand over to you practical plans for acquiring your goal. Hand over the thoughts to your imagination to create practical plans for the attainment of your ideal through transmutation of your desire. Do not wait for a definite plan but begin at once to see yourself in possession of your goal achieved, demanding and expecting meanwhile that your subconscious mind will hand over the plans you need. Be on the alert for these plans, and when they appear, put them into action immediately.

Autosuggestion to Improve your Self-Image

First. Go to some quiet spot, preferably in bed at night, close your eyes, and repeat aloud the written statement of the size you intend to become to be completely at ease to regain your self-confidence. As you do this, see yourself already in possession of your ideal body size. **Second.** Repeat this program night and morning until you can clearly visualize in your imagination who you intend to become. **Third**. Place a written copy of your statement where you can see it night and morning, and read it just before sleeping and first thing in the morning. Faith is the strongest and most productive of the emotions. This process may seem abstract. You can become the master of yourself and of your environment as you stay present because you absolutely have the power to influence your own subconscious mind and you can gain the cooperation of Infinite Intelligence.

- You have greatness Within You! It is possible to manifest your dreams! Is it difficult? Yes! and Is It Worth It? Yes! Be transformed by becoming a positive force in your own life. by Les Brown
- A burning desire to be and to do is the starting point from which a dreamer must take off & dreams are not born of indifference, laziness, or lack of ambition. – Napoleon Hill

II

PART

T: THE Imagination and Self-Reliance: You are your own best coach, you know yourself intimately better than anyone else knows you. Learn to teach your body ahead of time what your compelling future will feel like. Practice living in a state of grace, reach for the feelings of what it would be like to feel healthy and abundant to draw those states of being into your life!

- Your personality is how you think, act, and feel. To change your personal reality, you must change your personality. The secret then, is to teach your body ahead of time, what the future will feel like. Hold onto that feeling and get ready, that's when the magic happens! –Dr. Joe Dispenza
- Ideas are the beginning points of all successes. Ideas are products of the imagination. - Napoleon Hill

II

IMAGINATION
MY STORY

Hold it! 1, 2, 3 and down, and again, the burn in my abs and quads was excruciating during leg raises in dryland training as a freshman on the CU, Boulder recreation ski team. This was both the most exhilarating and challenging eight weeks of my life. I was the heaviest female by at least 40 pounds. I rode my bike to and from my dorm on sunny afternoons to lie down on the grass to do warmups beside some of the hottest athletes in Boulder, back in the day. The only way I could survive my inner torment of being so obviously out of place, in my thick leggings and tight long sleeves, while everyone else was in a tank and shorts or matching crop top and tights was to use what today, is my very best weapon, my imagination! I had the spirit and the work ethic to push my body but the only problem was that I had eaten all of my emotions over the last few years prior to reaching the university. I was so much bigger on the outside than the athlete I was in my heart! I felt ridiculously awkward and out of balance with who I was on the inside! After a humiliating moment, I went inside my head without realizing it, I said to myself, wait a sec, what if I tune into how my body is actually going through these motions? I focused on the mechanics of how my knees and my mind together could get my big butt up the long incline and down again to cycle these hill reps with the ski team! It was a pivotal moment for me. On our bikes, we did loops, pounding up the long but gradual incline as hard as we could, and then crouching down on the way down to practice gaining speed in a tuck the way we would do on snow a few months later. Decades before the rage of using a Peloton bike, we trained outdoors in any weather. I biked home from training that day, single file, with my quads burning and for the first time, I left feeling better than worse after the workout. Your mind is your own unique and free tool. Tapping into my imagination got me out of feeling debilitating mental embarrassment and pain. Continuing to focus on how my lungs responded to being at altitude, I remember biking up Flagstaff, at the base of the Rocky Mountains at a few body lengths behind a couple of dorm friends from my team. I had a crush on one of them so I was flattered to ride with them that day. The Flatirons are the base of the Rocky Mountains so I was both in awe of majestic view and in pain from really pushing my muscles that I knew were underneath the blubber on my legs. I used the same mind game as I did riding home from dry land training. I simply imagined how perfectly my quads, knees, and feet functioned to get me up the mountain. I was able to redirect my thoughts from feeling bad about eating or thinking about eating 24/7. I was able to lift the burden, a bit at a time. I started to make a point to tap into my imagination. What if I kept training consistently and stopped eating too much all the time, could I envision my legs truly deflating? Those questions were the first steps of my painless transformation without deprivation dieting. I began to watch my fat cells deflate. The number fat cells and their distribution on your body can grow but never decrease. You may have rolls in your mid-section, love handles or be like me, my knees are genetically super thick since I inherited fat stores in my knees and inner thighs. I mainly focus on imagining my muscular quads as ripped mostly since my legs are where most of my fat cells hang out together! Everyone is different, just go with what you were gifted, your miraculous body, and start to utilize your imagination as you practice this new way of looking at your body seeing what is underneath your currently swollen body. Every muscle fiber is there, working for you in perfect harmony with your heart and lungs. You can think of each fat cell as going from the swollen grapes to small marbles, depending on how much excess food each fat cell contains. It was empowering to shift away from my self-destructive thinking and fascinating to see real results over time. I stopped the midnight self-hatred binges for starters. I knew all about nutrition but the sheer number of calories from every bit of nervousness, newness, anxiety, happiness, joy, celebration, was more than I could burn off, even with dryland training. I developed the skill of forcing myself to stay deep inside my head, imagining my limbs and my swollen butt, literally deflating. The pivotal moment was when I committed to using my imagination in the mirror from that day forward. I never scrutinized or acknowledged what is there in the mirror. I only ever imagined what my physique looked and felt like as the ideal version of myself at my most comfortable size. This habit required me to develop self-reliance. I did not have the internet or a coach to give me feedback on my progress. I was becoming my biggest fan and my own best friend. Now it is 40 years later and I have transformed who I am on this planet, inside and out, using my best weapon, my imagination. I am sharing this with you so that you can start using your imagination today, in 5-minute windows, 24 hours at a time to fast track away from suffering and towards momentum!

- Be willing to dream, and imagine yourself becoming all that you wish to be. If you live from those imaginings, the universe will align with you in bringing all that you wish for- and even more than you imagined when you were living at an ordinary level of consciousness. –Dr. Wayne Dyer
- The only limitation is that which one sets up in one's own mind. - Napoleon Hill

The imagination is literally your workshop! Your impulse and desire takes shape, form, and action through the aid of your powerful and creative mind. Your thoughts can become things. We have discovered that our own brains are both a broadcasting and a receiving station for the vibration of thought. Your imaginative mind functions in two forms. One is the synthetic imagination and the other is the creative imagination. Your synthetic imagination is how you can arrange old concepts, ideas, or plans into new combinations. This creates nothing. It merely works with the material of your experience, education, and observation. Your creative imagination is the way your finite mind has direct communication with infinite intelligence. This is how hunches and inspirations reach your awareness. Thought vibrations or influences from the minds of others also come from using your creative imagination. This is the way that one individual may tune in or communicate with the subconscious minds of others. The creative imagination works automatically and only when the conscious mind is functioning at an exceedingly high level of intensity or energy. Your innate creative imagination becomes more alert and more receptive to influences in direct proportion to its development through use. By using both your synthetic and creative imagination, you become more alert and your skills will develop with use, just as any muscle or organ develops through use. You must remember to stay focused on you vs. you, not you vs. anyone else on the planet. If you spend your days going through the motions, guided by the emotions of your past, then your imagination has become weak through inaction. Your ability to become self-reliant is the catalyst for your real change. Your body is a miraculous machine and microscopic bits of matter have been organized and arranged in an orderly fashion. Every one of the billions of individual cells of your body began as an intangible form of energy. Nature has converted tiny cells into you as a complex, thinking, valuable, and unique human being. The conversion of your desire into its physical equivalent is just as miraculous! Do not become discouraged if this seems incomprehensible. It takes time to shift your daily thoughts, behaviors, and habits. The point is that your own creative imagination can take you from guilty and discouraged to hopeful and determined as you gain self-reliance and self-direction as you harness your desire and your powerful imagination. Leaning into your compelling future takes practice. You are essentially remembering your future.

- Identify your problems, but give your power and energy to solutions. -Tony Robbins
- Success requires no apologies, Failure permits no alibis. - Napoleon Hill
- By failing to prepare, you are preparing to fail. -Benjamin Franklin

ORGANIZED PLANNING
MY STORY

In 1983, at 3:58pm on a weekday, on the Boulder campus I was upbeat, with blubbery legs bouncing down the bright hallway of our dorm to meet my best friend to walk to the cafeteria when it opened for dinner at 4pm. We wanted to be there first, to get the freshest dorm food, if there was such a thing. We were able to make our choices before the hot items got cold or the cold items got to be lukewarm. That one hour each day meant so much to me with my new best friend. She was a talented sprinter from Albuquerque, NM and I admired her self-discipline and her physique. We became quick friends to travel to the weight room together 40 years ago, back in the day when women rarely went to the weight room. It was my first chance to get to know someone closely whose thoughtful planning of her meals gave her the results she was after as an athlete. I learned so much from her about not only what to eat but about making time to plan meals. It took years for me to embrace the lifestyle of taking the best care possible of the miraculous machine you have to mold and to understand that your body will respond exactly as you treat yourself. It was the first time I tried out organized planning. Desserts were my downfall so I decided to start there. To this day, I distinctly making the conscious choice of gearing up to fill my glass with crushed ice. Then from the dispenser, I watched myself fill the glass the rest of the way with chocolate milk and I grabbed a spoon. As I walked back to our table, I stayed focused on the exact dessert that I chose, not by impulse, but I actually planned on it ahead of time. I continued to surprise myself at my ability to plan my crushed ice, chocolate milk, and eat it with a spoon day after day. At first, I was astounded that I was capable of telling myself to plan to do something and then actually do it! It became a consistent thrill to choose and then enjoy my pre-planned choice of dessert while my best friend and I shared an hour or more chatting about our hopes and dreams for our college experience. The level of self-discipline it took me to do this one simple change to my 24 hours was astonishing. After this small win, for the first time I proved to myself that I could consistently follow my own directions! I left the cafeteria feeling the first ounce of pride in myself. It was a very unusual feeling. Right then I realized that if I made a plan for exactly what I would eat I could follow it. I did not have to give in to my emotions to inhale whatever I felt like consuming next without stopping when I got full. My light bulb moment came one afternoon asking myself, What if I tried to organize and plan more of my meals ahead of time and actually followed through with my plan. As a reminder, this was years before the internet where you have access to so many weight loss plans and fitness gurus in the palm of your hand. I had my best friend as living proof of the results of thinking more correctly by planning what to eat ahead of time. Respecting your body by eating more correctly, it is possible to see the rewards. I believe that her self-respect towards her athletic body was what I admired the most. She led by example of how to really look inward, to slow down, and to organize your eating habits. After decades of adopting new habits, I was able to re-channel my intensity towards food by really concentrating on making the most correct next choice. I had no idea of the positive impact it would make by me deliberately and carefully choosing ahead of time exactly what I would put into my body. This gave me back a sense of self-control that in turn lifted my inner shame and stress that in turn lifted the weight of the world off my mind. For years leading up to that fall in the cafeteria my mood triggered my intake of food or drinks I never took the time to think and plan, ever. I felt just like a cow grazing since I ate by my moods, never stopping when my stomach felt full. The feeling of being full as a signal to stop eating was irrelevant most of the time, for decades. It was a painful way to cope. Beginning in 1964, when I was young, I grew up having dessert after every family meal. Knowing you are an emotional eater is when many other facets of your life are easily, even rigidly easily under your control but when it comes to the fridge and cupboard of carbs there is no restraint whatsoever! At my heaviest when I was unorganized in terms of not planning any of my meals, I started by focusing on only the very next 24 hours. I made a plan to burn off more than I took in for just the next 24 hours. The easiest start to my plan was to replace sugary soda, caffeine, and fruit juices with clear liquids that had zero calories. For some reason, this was the easiest way for me not to feel deprived to be able to cut way down on empty calories the quickest. I realized that I had been drinking a ton of empty calories. After school on the way to track practice, I began choosing to drink the bottled water that I brought from home, instead of a coke from the vending machine to copy the cool kids' choices right after the final bell rang at the end of the school day! From there, I gained momentum and kept it up to reach an elevated and wholly new state of being. It is so rewarding and hopeful to practice feeling more abundant each day. On restrictive diets I simply felt deprived and could not handle waiting for my stomach to grumble to ask myself what I'm going to eat next. That was my biggest mistake for so many years. All day, every day, as I slow down instead of eating on every impulse I learned to rely on myself to plan correctly and I keep real food in the fridge. I have successfully deflated my swollen fat cells by using organized planning 24 hours at a time. Thinking ahead by one day, where will I be, what times will I have the opportunity to eat? What are my choices? Will I need to stop to buy something at my mealtime? Where will I buy my meal? My focus lately being stuck at home during the pandemic for two years, has shifted to what can I take in to feel the best after I eat and what do I need to drink to go along with what I take in? I get very specific ahead of time, every single day. Planning is the key since every day is different, like a workday, with a commute or if I work from home, a weekend, a holiday, etc. On a side note, at 57, my body seems to no longer have the ability to digest alcohol, my body treats it like liquid fat, I wake up bloated, not feeling well, so that's rarely even a choice I make on a holiday any more. It does take time to plan but as emotional eaters how rewarding on our finite journey on this planet to feel better 24 hours from now than you do now as you persistently make better choices. You will feel organized which will give you momentum and a feeling of control. It all started as the game of replacement behaviors! You cannot quit eating your favorite foods or reach you goal by sheer deprivation dieting unless suffering is your thing! One replacement behavior after another and you can feel your inner momentum and your mood improve! Long-term success at deflating, as I like to call it, takes consistent organized planning. Micro-progress IS progress. You and your body are the only ones who need to know you are about to embark on a personal journey of transformation. How exciting to have no more ridicule or get unsolicited advice from your relatives who are not emotionally connected to food like we are! This journey is all you vs. you. I am your catalyst for real change!

Planning helps you in so many ways as an emotional eater. You must be sick and tired of being sick and tired of being uncomfortable in your skin, if your discomfort is solely the result of you eating all the wrong things to curb every emotion. Sluggish and worn down is not the only way to go through your days, even though you may use food as your only go-to. I understand, I was and am the same way, to this day! Please know that your organized food plan for the next 24 hours, the food and drinks you select are as unique as you are! If I had to cut out cheese, there would be zero impact, why? I hate cheese and I never eat it! Skippy super chunk peanut butter? Well let's just say if I'm in a hurry to lose a pound or two that would be the first thing I cut out since I eat so much of it on celery. My point is that your plan has to relate to your current habits and lifestyle. If the first plan you adopt does not work successfully, replace it with a new plan. If that new plan fails to work, replace it with still another and so on until you find a plan that does work without strict deprivation. Most people who fail only do so because of their lack of persistence in creating new plans to implement for the next 24 hours. You will become a role model to your loved ones who may still be suffering as emotional eaters themselves. Your transformation will be a better feeling than you can even imagine at this moment! It is real and it is possible for you. Since you turn to food to alleviate every single emotion, to re-channel that intensity by simply planning you are proving to yourself that you are capable of regaining self-control.

- Plan your work for today and every day, then work your plan. –Margaret Thatcher
- Taking massive action, learning from what doesn't work, changing your approach until you get to what you want is really what makes someone succeed long term in any context. –Tony Robbins
- If you would like a more abundant life, then you must believe in yourself, and not rely on others for encouragement or support. Sounds harsh, but it is your path to freedom. – Dean Grasiosi
- Our goals can only be reached through the vehicle of a plan. There is no other route to success. –Pablo Picasso

ORGANIZED PLANNING
NAPOLEON HILL'S STRATEGY
APPLIED TO EMOTIONAL EATING

To reach a personal goal your plans must be practical and workable. Temporary defeat should only mean one thing- the certain knowledge that there is something wrong with your plan. Quitting in your own mind is the only real defeat. It is so easy to give up on yourself at the first sign of defeat. For people who have achieved their personal goal we often recognize only their triumph overlooking the temporary setbacks they had to overcome along the way. If you give up before your goal is attained you are a quitter, that is only defeat in your mind. As you learn to strategically plan your own shifts in behavior remember that there are reasons you have become so completely out of touch with yourself. It is not your fault! It is simply that your constant conditioning and emotional triggers are all around you all day. You have not made time to make a solid plan ahead of time. A lack of ambition to aim above mediocrity may be the reason you were so stifled for so long, simply eating all of your emotions. Your body is a miraculous machine and when you realize it, you will begin to treat yourself with more respect. Give yourself the opportunity to make time to introduce structure that was missing by planning replacements and better food choices. It is fascinating as you slow down, to watch your body respond as you improve in 5-minute windows, 24 hours at a time. The way your body takes in, digests, and utilizes nutrients can be a fascinating journey if you give yourself the chance to succeed by having the patience. It requires you to plan your meals 24 hours at a time. Discipline comes from self-control. Before you control your conditions, you must first control yourself. Self-mastery is the hardest job you will ever tackle! You may see at the same time both your best friend and your greatest enemy by stepping in front of a mirror. As your habits improve and planning becomes less of a burden, the feeling can be extraordinary. Most of us are good starters, but poor finishers of everything we begin. Moreover, people are prone to give up at the first sign of defeat. There is no substitute for persistence. Failure cannot cope with persistence. People who succeed reach decisions promptly and change them, if at all, very slowly. People who fail reach decisions, if at all, very slowly and change them quickly and frequently. Indecision and procrastination are twins that will kill any sense of real progress that you want to make on your quest to look and feel better. Enthusiasm on the other hand is contagious. This means that as you start to show outwardly that you are enthusiastic towards this day and your ability to improve, that energy will be felt by your spouse, your friends, and if you have children, that will be the most rewarding start to your journey! Children feel your unspoken energy and lack of enthusiasm whether you like it or not! Be the role model you want during these next few critical years, simply by elevating your self-talk and practicing enthusiasm towards your ability to learn what it takes to progress! Most people are too indifferent or lazy to acquire facts with which to think accurately. They prefer to act on opinions created by guesswork or snap-judgements. You are worth so much more than any mean judgement placed on yourself for your poor habits when it comes to self-control in the kitchen. You can never stop thinking about what you will take in next, which you can truly flip into your superpower! As you develop on your journey of self-awareness, focusing and controlling your next choice of what you take in, it elevates your state of being. You will radiate self-confidence, self-respect, and dignity just by staying focused on your thoughts, behaviors, in 5-minute windows, 24 hours at a time. The older you get the more quickly and easily your body reacts to your good or bad choice of what you put into your body. This sounds counter-intuitive. Your body is more sensitive to changes so you will feel better quicker if you begin your journey of transformation later in life. It is never too late to improve upon the choices of what you put into your body. Your ability to correctly plan is a way to get started on your deeply personal journey towards the person you intend to become! It is possible for you to stop suffering as you begin to make organized plans. One thing though, it is no longer ok to dream and to dabble! You have the potential to surprise yourself as your body goes from being your worst enemy to your best friend, you may just not feel it yet!

- There are dreamers and there are planners; the planners make their dreams come true. -Edwin Louis Cole.
- Nothing great was ever achieved without enthusiasm. -Ralph Waldo Emerson
- If you are not willing to learn, no one can help you. If you are determined to learn, no one can stop you. -Zig Ziglar

DECISION
MY STORY

It was a dreary weekday morning at the table, before school, pondering my day ahead, when I made a conscious decision to choose to eat fruit and toast instead of two heaping bowls of sugary cereal. I made the decision right then as I made the decision to make better choices of what to put into my body next! I started slowly because to restrict my intake felt like I was starving! I knew that I was obsessed with food since I used it to curb every emotion so to stop consuming refined sugar was not even an option at the time. I realize now that I was setting myself up to fail at every new fad diet that came along. Back before the internet, we only had television, radio, or word of mouth to hear about any new diet craze. In my mind, I believed I was doomed because I knew myself and understood that since I thought about food 24/7 that I would never succeed at any kind of restrictive diet. I started very slowly, beginning with breakfast at my first attempt on my long journey of replacement behaviors. I decided that I would attempt to make micro-progress because I was extremely uncomfortable in my body. It was miraculous to look in the mirror and to begin to watch the swelling of my thunder thighs go down. At first, though, I could only see that I was making better choices at the table. Over time, I was able to see and feel the results of making better choices. I made the committed decision to begin and continue making replacement behaviors in regards to what I took in at each meal and then I improved at what I ate in between meals as well. I learned to appreciate that fact that your body is a miraculous machine. It is yours and you are in control over the choices you make even though most choices you make about food are emotionally charged. That makes sense, but you are still in control over those choices. Since your body is a machine it must respond to exactly what you take in and how you treat yourself. I decided to improve my choices and start speaking to myself with more respect that got easier as I gained momentum in my ability to make better choices. I started to believe in myself again and my ability to trust myself to make the less poor choice when I had options of what to eat next. I consciously decided to repeat this process in 5-minute windows, 24 hours at a time. I did this consistently for the most part, all day every day for over three decades. I was able to drop and keep off over 10 sizes by not depriving myself of food, ever. Instead, over time, I continued to decide to pick the better option and my body responded correctly. It was truly miraculous to think of how making a decision can change your life forever. For me, making the decision to make a point to select the better option at mealtime was the trick. I never felt deprived in any environment no matter how different the situation was when it came to my next meal. It was obvious which choice would make more sense. Years into my journey choosing the better option was a personal game that became fun! You can progress to the point where I am today of deciding to only take in nutrients that I know my body can use. I have evolved to the point of giving up most empty calories and it shows! It is thrilling to me to look in the mirror and see the results of treating my body with dignity after deciding decades ago to make better choices when it came time to eat my next meal. My future is no longer discouraging, it is hopeful! By deciding to focus on your next choice, in 5-minute windows,

24 hours at a time, you will see results in your glorious machine that is your body. As you practice self-control, you will grow completely away from feeling shame and self-defeat as you stop storing empty calories because your body will utilize the nutrients you take in!

- It is in your moments of decision that your destiny is shaped. -Tony Robbins
- No one can see your personal decisions, they only see the results of your decisions. The principle of decision-making is to decide right where you are with whatever you've got and to never let circumstances permit you from making a decision. – Bob Proctor
- Go confidently in the direction of your dreams! Live the life you have imagined.-Henry David Thoreau

DECISION
NAPOLEON HILL'S STRATEGY
APPLIED TO EMOTIONAL EATING

Lack of decision is the major cause of failure. Procrastination, the opposite of decision is a common enemy that practically every individual must conquer. You will have an opportunity to test your capacity to reach quick and definite decisions when you finish reading this and you are ready to begin putting these principles into action. Take no one into your confidence except those who are in complete sympathy and harmony with your purpose. Close friends and relatives while not meaning to do so often handicap you through opinions and sometimes ridicule which they meant to be humorous. You have a brain and a mind of your own. Use it to reach your own decisions. Genuine wisdom is usually conspicuous through modesty and silence. These laws are available to every person who has the faith and courage to use them. Just take the time necessary to understand and apply them. Those who reach decisions promptly and definitely know what they want and generally get it. The world has a habit of making room for those individuals whose words and actions show that they know where they are going. Indecision is a bad habit that usually begins when you are young. The habit takes on permanency over time so you wake up one day without definiteness of purpose. It is not your fault if you were never encouraged to practice the habit of making definite decisions. That habit always requires courage since it requires you to expect, plan, and raise your standards.

- Once you make a decision, the universe conspires to make it happen. -Ralph Waldo Emerson
- You and only you are responsible for your life choices and decisions. -Robert T. Kiyosaki
- The right decisions are always the hardest to make but they must be made in order to live the life you deserve. - Trent Shelton

M: MOMENT, Self-Talk in the Now:

Your subconscious cannot reject any idea you give to it. Learn to reach for better feeling thoughts and words to describe yourself in the 12-60,000 thoughts you have each day. Learn to combine a clear intention with an elevated emotion to improve how you think, act, and feel by determining what you really, really want!

- They Are Able Who Think They Are Able. – Virgil
- Patience, persistence, and perspiration make an unbeatable combination for success. – Napoleon Hill
- God seems to throw Himself on the side of the individual who knows exactly what they want if they are determined to get just that! –Napoleon Hill

PERSISTENCE
MY STORY

Persistence has been the most important tool in my tool kit since I first started thinking about the possibility that I could slim down if I made better decisions. I ate all of my emotions and gained weight at a time in history before the internet was invented, before everyone carried a cell phone, if you can imagine that, so I had no way to seek out immediate support for my insecurities from social media. For that reason, I felt very alone with my emotional eating habits because I only had peers who were what I thought of as normal meaning their average sizes reflected their ability to stop eating when they were full. I spent a lot of time inside my head most of the time. Since I felt like I was the only person who thought about food 24/7 it was a lonely and painful time in my life. Before I made the decision to make replacement behaviors a priority, I went way inside my mind one evening as I started to ponder the possibility of whether there was any possibility that I could be persistent in having any self-control whatsoever? Could I possibly have the discipline to play the game of reducing my portion sizes? Portion control was a drastically new idea to be honest, back in 1980. This was about the time that I first acknowledged that the amount of extra food I took in all day every day was the source of my size and my perpetual discomfort. I was truly in denial and I just knew I felt intense emotions and that food comforted me to get to the next hour. I knew there was no way I could ever go without all the foods and candy that I loved so much. I truly knew that I had zero willpower to deprive myself of anything, ever. Food was my punishment and my reward because I realize now that I never just ate to satisfy hunger. I can honestly say that I revolved my entire young adult life around feeding my emotions. Once I admitted that I never just ate because I was hungry, at least I had a baseline. As a junior in high school, my normal routine involved eating until the point where my stomach ached, which was way after I got full. Our family mealtime together was a very emotionally charged nightly event. There were unwritten very high expectations for my achievement and I definitely made it more intense for myself. I suppose, looking back, most of the pressure I felt was self-inflicted to perform academically by getting great grades. To strive for perfection and for my parents approval, kept me inside my head, if that makes sense. The high emotional charge it took to stay driven was a lot to handle. One school night, I had a profound thought as I was plodding down the plush carpeted steps, stopping in the middle of doing homework to join my family for dinner. As I came around the corner and approached the wonderful smells at the table, I felt a wave of hope and excitement as I decided ahead of time that I would show some restraint by playing a game and cut my portion sizes down in half. I then inhaled half and then picked at the second half, ending up eating three quarters of what was on my plate. I must admit, that was a huge accomplishment for me at the time. There was no way in the world I was going to deprive myself of any fatty favorite foods so I began to try to make a game out of practicing my portion control to earn a tiny win. Over time, persistence at my portion control became a more natural habit. My self-discipline got better because I was not depriving myself of foods that I loved since I was simply stopping before I felt distended and gross. Even at family events and holiday parties, everywhere food was served I was able to play this new game with myself. I got better at deciding ahead of time that I would make a point to reduce my portions, of whatever was coming at me next. Gatherings and parties always served buffet style food so to me that meant no limits for the longest time. Then with persistence, I was able to serve myself a heaping plate just like everyone else. Then, I started to get better at eating half of what was on my plate. This mental challenge became rewarding which gave me momentum as I attempted my secret first steps to self-control. I would never be able to deprive myself, ever. Persistence will pay off for you in a very real way over time, unlike deprivation dieting. I was learning with myself as the guinea pig, exactly how my body responded as my fat cells deflated over time. My face, my round German nose, my arms, and eventually my legs were less swollen which was a real boost to my self-confidence. I started to be proud of myself again, inside my heart. I had proven to myself that through persistence not by deprivation that our human body as a miraculous machine does in fact respond to exactly how you treat it. One key point is that because I was so emotionally attached to food, I knew that I could not focus on beyond the next 24 hours at any one time. I would get overwhelmed at how far I had to go so I stuck to portion control for a long time, and the results were rewarding. You can learn to be persistent and it is not something you have to discuss with the people around you unless you feel like it. Your quest for self-improvement will only ever be you vs. you and it is a deeply personal journey. By really getting granular, leaning into the present moment is all you need to stop suffering. Starting in 5-minute windows, 24 hours at a time, concentrating on your next choice of what to take in and how much to take in is the trick. Motivation to stay focused requires a strong reason why. If you do not feel motivated to start to try yet, you can use the notion of wanting to stop feeling bloated and over-full as a very simple reason to attempt portion control at your next meal. It took me a long time to get good at persistence and at managing portion control but it does not have to take you as long to gather momentum. That is my hope for you as I share my true-life experiences with you. As an emotional eater, it is your superpower to learn to re-channel your intensity towards making the best next choice, starting with not finishing your entire plate and going for seconds or thirds. You get to start right now! Your self-esteem and self-reliance will improve as you continue to have little wins. This will give you momentum to stay persistent. Understanding that you have what it takes to begin to start to exhibit persistency is very hopeful on your journey back to self-love. Over three decades I have successfully raised my standards. Persistently retraining your thinking to stay in the now is exactly what it takes to start to feel better since there is no better feeling than being in control of your thoughts, behaviors, and habits. Learning consistency and understanding that your body has to respond correctly when you make small improvements in your routines is key. You will also get better at positive reinforcement of your own messages as you guide yourself through each day. It is too hard to think about what my choices might be tomorrow or next week, I feel completely overwhelmed and immobilized if I think too far ahead. Micro-progress by focusing on your very next choice has a significant impact on how you feel afterwards. Stay granular, stay present. You can focus and gather momentum 24 hours at a time no matter how old you are and that is the most exciting part about giving yourself permission to do the best you know how. It truly took me decades to absorb to my core the value of persistence. As they say, hindsight is 20/20. I am writing this as living proof that if you lean into persistence, never giving up on your body as a fascinating machine, you can wake up in a year from now with a new outlook on life and your future! Your body can become your very best friend, someone you love and respect and treat with the utmost kindness. You will solidify your inner power! You will restore your self-worth and self-confidence instead of repeating the same old habit of punishing yourself for those extra trips to the fridge. It does take consistency and persistence to feel and see results so you must be okay with taking baby steps at first. Portion control is one of the first things to try on your deeply personal journey back to yourself. If you have been eating all of your emotions for years then by now your body reflects it and you are super uncomfortable with the size of your body. You may be much bigger than you ever thought you would be at your age. Your time is now literally if you are conscious, you can use the power of Now. You can learn to master the moment! As you self-reflect and grow in your awareness that you do eat all of your emotions, like I always will, and there is no way to get over being this way so understand this connection is yours to redirect into your superpower! These tools are free, so let yourself start right here, right now to use the next 5-minutes to your advantage! Your journey away from self-defeat to self-acceptance on your way to being self-driven start now. Your body is your machine to control by changing your thinking. Portion control and replacement behaviors are mind games that you get to play without the embarrassment of anyone else knowing what you are doing, unless you want them to know. You are not stuck! This moment is all you have and all you will ever need to change your future!

- Without making the actual attempt, without trial and strife, there can be no true knowledge, no progress, no high achievement, and no legend. –Brendon Burchard
- Never bend your head. Always hold it high. Look the world straight in the eye. –Helen Keller
- When [negative]thoughts and feelings that used to signal the body are stopped by your conscious efforts, the liberated energy from those limited emotions is released into the field. You now have energy with which to design and create a new destiny. –Dr. Joe Dispenza

PERSISTENCE
NAPOLEON HILL'S STRATEGY
APPLIED TO EMOTIONAL EATING

There is no substitute for persistence! In the beginning it may seem difficult and slow. Persistence is a state of mind and you will be rewarded for your persistence over time.

Factors of Persistence

1. Definiteness of purpose. Knowing what you want is the first and perhaps, the most important step toward the development of persistence. A strong motive forces you to surmount many difficulties.
2. Desire. It is comparatively easy to acquire and to maintain persistence in pursuing the object of intense desire.
3. Self-reliance. Belief in your ability to carry out a plan encourages you to follow the plan through with persistence.
4. Definiteness of plans.
5. Organized plans, even though they may be weak and impractical at first.
6. Accurate knowledge. Knowing that your plans are sound, based upon experience or observation.
7. Cooperation. Sympathy, understanding, and harmonious cooperation with others tends to develop persistence.
8. Will power. The habit of concentrating your thoughts on building plans to have a definite goal and purpose.
9. Habit. Persistence is the direct result of habit. Your mind absorbs and becomes a part of the daily experiences upon which it feeds. You can overcome fear as you repeat acts of courage.

The Symptoms of Lack of Persistence

If you have any of these symptoms, they are deep in your subconscious and these traits must be overcome in order for you to reach your goal:

1. Indecision. The habit of passing the buck on all occasions instead of facing issues squarely.
2. The habit of relying upon alibis instead of creating definite plans for solutions of problems.
3. Self-satisfaction. There is but little remedy for this affliction and no hope for giving in to it.
4. Indifference. Readiness to compromise rather than meet opposition and fight it.
5. The habit of blaming others for one's mistakes and poor choices.
6. Weakness of desire, from not having a strong enough Why.
7. Willingness, even eagerness to quit at the first sign of defeat.

8. Lack of organized plans, placed in writing to see them and review them.
9. The habit of neglecting to take action on good ideas or grasp opportunity when it presents itself.
10. Wishing instead of willing.
11. The habit of staying lazy instead of choosing to begin to act.
12. Searching for all the shortcuts to weight loss, without understanding that your body is a machine and you must treat it correctly, with respect, period.
13. Fear of criticism, which leads to failure to create plans and put them into action. Fear of criticism can be stronger than the desire for success because you fear the criticism of relatives and friends who tell you not to aim so high or they will think you are crazy.

How To Develop Persistence

1. A definite purpose backed by a burning desire for its fulfillment.
2. A definite plan, expressed in continuous action.
3. A mind closed tightly against all negative and discouraging influences, including negative suggestions of relatives, friends and acquaintances.
4. A friendly alliance with one or more people who will encourage you to follow through with both plan and purpose.
   - No thought, whether it be negative or positive, can enter the subconscious mind without the principle of Autosuggestion. - Napoleon Hill
   - Stay focused. Your start does not determine how you're going to finish. -Herm Edwards
   - If you have a positive attitude and constantly strive to give your best effort, eventually you will overcome your immediate problems. -Pat Riley

It was the end of the fourth quarter and there I was at mid-field with the soccer ball in my possession. I looked up with determination and the skinny center forward on the opposing team actually stepped out of my way. With no hesitation, I put some muscle into it and yes, I scored from midfield. My own center fielder who I usually pass to for her to score cheered for me loudly. It seemed like a proud moment. Deep down, I was actually mortified at the size of my thunder thighs in my yellow polyester shorts with bright wide stripes along the edges. I felt ashamed at how bulky and uncomfortable it felt to plod across the field to receive praise from my coach. I cried inside all the way home after the game. I was glad to help our team win but deep down I knew that I was only that powerful on the field from eating all of my emotions for a couple of years straight. By the time I was a senior in high school, I carried the heavy burden of my thick thighs clearly in my mind and in my awkward appearance. The only image I had in my mind of my thick legs was exactly what I saw in the mirror. I gazed into the mirror and confirmed that there I saw the ice cream, the chips, the pizza, and the cookies, in grape size dimples of fat on my thighs. It was humiliating deep down to have that image in my subconscious mind. I held that image of myself firmly in my mind. I woke up feeling bulky and bummed out as I constantly reminded myself of how awful I looked and felt. The day had not started yet but I reinforced my thoughts of feeling heavy like lead all day. I consistently went to bed feeling worse than when I woke up for rebranding my current image of my body into my brain. The shame and the burden of carrying so much extra weight, for me, became a real nuisance. I ran out of energy quickly. I was going to go to college the following year so I do not know the exact moment but I woke up one day, craving to feel better. I began to use my full-length mirror to visualize my body starting with my legs as deflated with tone not just buried in bulk. The most valuable time in 24 hours that I used was on my way to sleep. I started recreating the picture in my mind that I had of my body. I pretended that I was lean and comfortable in my skin. I tried to visualize what I looked like underneath the extra fat cells that I remembered would never go away but could shrink in size. The pivotal moment I reached was deep in my thoughts, late at night, cozy under the covers. I started seeing my body as my ideal size in my mind and that was step one. I woke up feeling a bit less awkward. I started holding the picture in my mind of my muscles being strong and smooth when I walked, not heavy and bulky. I do not ever use the word fat to describe myself or anyone since fat is a thing, a noun, fat is not an adjective to describe yourself. The function of your fat cells store is to hold the excess food that you do not burn off during your day. You are a human being so that is how your body works on purpose which is a good thing! As I continued to visualize my ideal image of my body very clearly in my mind, I started to act accordingly. My thoughts and behavior improved to match my improved self-image which I held deep in my subconscious mind. I started to burn off more than I took in every 24 hours. It was not such a trudge to walk down the halls to class anymore. I was still uncomfortably big relative to my own standards. I felt differently about my body in my mind and I am sure that was the reason that I continued to progress to reach my goal of dropping 10 sizes without depriving myself of my favorite foods or any nonsense. I simply spent much more time acting as if I was already at my goal. I started thinking, acting, and feeling as if I was already where I wanted to be physically more often each day, especially on my way to sleep. This took commitment since it was so foreign to me but I kept up this new way of thinking since it made me feel better! I was used to reaching for a more self-debilitating thought than the one I just had to spiral my thoughts downward until I fell asleep immobilized by my negative self-talk. This was such a painful memory and I share it to give you hope in knowing that there is so much room for improvement as you talk yourself to sleep. Years later, beginning in 2005 when YouTube was invented I watched everything I could find about self-talk and visualization. Prior to then, I learned these secrets of success the hard way, all on my own. You do not have to spend another minute suffering with a bad self-image. Close your eyes for a moment to go inside your mind and force yourself to create a new picture of yourself right now or as soon as you have a few moments alone. It costs nothing. No one needs to know that you are actively redefining the image you hold of yourself in your subconscious mind. Practicing the valuable skill of feeding your subconscious mind the image of exactly who you intend to become, in every single detail is the most effective path out of suffering as an emotional eater. It takes effort to repeat this regularly but is doable for you. It is time to paint a clear picture of yourself in your subconscious mind so strongly that you are able to "Act as if…"any time you feel like it, from now on! We cannot outperform our self-image, as said by Maxwell Maltz. Therefore, we must first clearly define ourselves in our subconscious mind. Whichever diet or exercise how to plan you may choose to follow after reading this will only work as well as you remember to hold on tight to your ideal image of yourself in your mind as often as possible. Lean into that feeling and hold it in your mind ideally first thing in the morning and on your way to sleep at night. No one around you needs to know that this elevated way of thinking is your new secret weapon of success! You will gradually feel less overwhelmed by the choices you made in your past that got you to this point of discomfort and guilt. You absolutely get a fresh start each new day. As long as you work hard at improving your inner dialogue, you will be on your way to hope and renewed excitement. As you learn to utilize your subconscious mind as a powerful tool, you will have begun your deeply personal journey of transformation.

- The most important conversation is the one you have with yourself. –David Goggins
- A higher concept of yourself involves taking on new truths and shedding your old views of what you can achieve. This is the only way you can achieve your desires. You must begin by replacing your old set of truths with a belief in the existence of a higher self within you. –Dr. Wayne Dyer
- All individuals have become what they are because of their dominating thoughts and desires. –Napoleon Hill

Your subconscious mind is active all the time, it works day and night. Your subconscious mind draws upon the forces of Infinite Intelligence for the power with which it voluntarily transmutes your desires into the physical equivalent. This happens as you make use of the most practical plan by which this end may be accomplished using the connecting link between the finite human mind and Infinite Intelligence. Once you have accepted the reality of the existence of your subconscious mind and understand its possibilities, you will also understand the necessity of persistence in carrying out instructions.

Remember that your subconscious mind can be directed only through habit, using the faith in your ability to improve as you give yourself permission to go into your mind and elevate your feelings. It takes time to master faith in yourself and in your body's ability to respond as you make new choices and think deeper thoughts about your potential and the ideal image of your body that would like to attain. Be Patient. Be Persistent. Your subconscious mind functions automatically so any thoughts of fear and self-defeat get into your subconscious mind unless you master these impulses. It understands the language of emotion or feeling. These are the feelings to feed your subconscious mind:

The Seven Major Positive Emotions

- The emotion of DESIRE
- The emotion of FAITH
- The emotion of LOVE
- The emotion of SEX
- The emotion of ENTHUSIASM
- The emotion of ROMANCE
- The emotion of HOPE

Positive and negative emotions cannot occupy the mind at the same time. It is your responsibility to learn to shift your focus away from these feelings:

The Seven Major Negative Emotions

- The emotion of FEAR
- The emotion of JEALOUSY
- The emotion of HATRED

- The emotion of REVENGE
- The emotion of GREED
- The emotion of SUPERSTITION
- The emotion of ANGER

By habit, your positive emotions can dominate your mind so completely that the negatives cannot enter it. This is the best way to gain control of your subconscious mind. The highest form of energy known is the energy of thought! Thought vibrations and energy connects every human brain with other human brain. In addition, this is the connection between the finite human mind and Infinite Intelligence. This kind of communication requires patience, faith, persistence, and a deep desire to feel and look better!

- The best is yet to be. –Robert Browning
- One of our greatest gifts is our intuition. It is a sixth sense we all have – we just need to learn to tap into and trust it. –Donna Karan

In the late summer of 2018, while I was flat on my back in excruciating pain recovering from my TKR, *total knee replacement* of my right knee I started watching YouTube as a distraction from the pain. I found Tom Bilyeu, of Impact Theory, who interviewed David Goggins whose one nugget that resonated with me was that "on the other side of suffering is greatness." I watched that interview on a loop for five weeks with a deep sense of hope that his message would be true for me. Hope was better than despair and I spent the hot summer in bed with my knee bent resting on the air conditioner unit in the window to elevate it and to alleviate the excruciating pain. The prescribed opioids worked for me worked but when it came time to refill the prescription, I decided to not do so. I was wary of continuing to take such a strong medicine. I was truly afraid of never coming down from that zone if I continued to take the pills daily for another four weeks. I chose to experience the pain of recovery from surgery and it was much worse than it would have been on pain meds. I have an undiagnosed but certainly an obsessive compulsive and addictive personality, so it was a very real fear that I could have become obsessed with wanting the euphoric state of mind to continue beyond the length of my refill. My recovery was slow and painful and then I seem to have recovered exponentially. I came so far in the few years following my surgery that now it feels amazing to have a bionic knee. My physical limits are up to me again instead of limited by knee pain. After the last three years of deliberate self-talk, hours of stretching, and the newfound courage and pain-free existence, I could comfortably run at the track and spin on my stationary bike in a full range of movement and without pain. When you have been in chronic pain for weeks, nothing compares to being out of pain. I am a fan of Tom Bilyeu who hosts video interviews to discuss human potential with people who are fully devoted to their area of chosen expertise. He shares that as a human it is fascinating that you are truly malleable. You can deliberately decide to change your goals and objectives as you age. You have the ability to decide to live your life on purpose. You can even pick one thing and spend your life "raging to master" as Tom Bilyeu says, whatever you decide to commit to in order to live a more fulfilling life. You have a unique gift to share with the world you may just not know what it is yet.

I plan on empowering emotional eaters who are suffering with poor self-esteem, low self-reliance, and debilitating self-talk by explaining the value of focusing on your choices in the next 5-minute window, 24 hours at a time. You can create your future regardless of how you look and feel today. Your past brought you to this point but your past does not control your thoughts, behaviors, and actions of your future. Being a deeply emotional eater is your superpower, not something you need to stop. You can have fun with your intuition, by giving yourself permission to re-channel that intense emotional connection to food by pouring energy into making the next correct choice of what to eat. It is time for you to give yourself permission to think differently as you learn to master the moment! I have lived this truth for the last 40 years, as you cut down on your self-debilitating self-talk by practicing self-reliance and by flipping those nasty comments around, by reaching for a better feeling thought you truly can begin to look and feel better! At 57, I have come full circle emotionally. As a child, I was carefree, athletic, and my body felt amazing. 50 years later, I once again feel athletic and my body feels fantastic. I am at ease in my body, relatively thin by my own standards, and that matters most of all because I stay in tune with my intuition. My intuition guides me to make my next choice in the next 5-minute window, meaning is the result of my choice going to help me feel better or worse than I do right now? Thin is a relative term to refer to your own body at your most comfortable size not thin compared to anyone else. I need you to grasp the power and the magic of retraining your thinking.

I moved to New England right in time for the harsh winters and for puberty that felt like an emotional rollercoaster and I alleviated every emotion with food. The newness of eating so much to calm new feelings of my hormones was the beginning of my long journey from self-loathing to self-acceptance to self-love. Having the internet and an IPhone to access valuable content from thought leaders around the world at every moment were extraordinary tools that became accessible during my lifetime. Your own sense of dignity and self-respect come from trusting your intuition consistently to make correct choices of what to take in next, not by comparing yourself to someone online who may be much farther along on their journey or be using filters to improve your perception of them. True self-confidence and inner joy is possible as you spend more time deep in your mind reaching for a better feeling thought as much as possible. You can reach a state of being of gratitude and self-love. As you improve your thoughts, behaviors, and habits, your body will to go from being your worst enemy to your very best friend!

Dr. Joe Dispenza, neuroscientist, is passionate about teaching meditation as a way to lean into your compelling future. He collided with a car in the bike portion of a triathlon. He put his vertebrae back together, one by one, lying in a hospital bed, in his mind. He explained that as you work towards the goal of brain and heart coherence, by consciously combining a clear intention with an elevated emotion, you feel better and the result is a more positive state of being. I first learned of Dr. Joe and his teachings during my knee surgery recovery in 2018. I focused solely on teaching my body emotionally what my pain free knees would feel like ahead of time. It was tough but it was excellent practice. Thinking differently is a learned skill and your choice! You can learn to master the moment!

- You have power over your mind - not outside events. Realize this, and you will find strength. -Marcus Aurelius
- High performance is not about getting ahead at all costs. It's about forming habits that help you both excel in and enrich the full spectrum of your life. - Brendon Burchard

III PART

THE SIXTH SENSE
NAPOLEON HILL'S STRATEGY
APPLIED TO EMOTIONAL EATING

The greatest forces are intangible. The world is gathering an understanding of the forces that are intangible and unseen. You may be starting to learn and understand that your other self is more powerful than the physical self you see when you look in the mirror. The sixth sense is that portion of the subconscious mind that has been associated with your creative imagination. It is how ideas, plans, and thoughts flash into your mind, called hunches or inspirations. Understanding of the sixth sense comes only from meditation through mind development from within. The sixth sense most likely is the medium of contact between the finite mind and Infinite Intelligence to transmute desires into material form. You have become exactly what you are today because of your dominating thoughts and desires. One blessing of maturity is the courage to be truthful. As we age, the spiritual forces related to your sixth sense become easier to use through meditation, self-examination, and serious thought. You cannot outperform your deepest self-image. It takes focus and inner drive to develop to the point of having perspective on yourself. The fact is that deep inner work is required if you are ever to make real change.

AFTERWORD

The first step of your inner work is practicing patience and respect for yourself as a miracle for simply existing as a human being. At times of frustration, it is a fun challenge to re-direct your angst and intensity towards making the best choice in your next 5-minute window of time. I am sharing my methodology to empower you as an emotional eater, to give you the jumpstart on your inner work beginning with your first challenge of flipping your negative self-talk on its head. You have 12-60,000 thoughts in a day. This is your opportunity to begin to start to try to be nicer to yourself for the next 5-minutes, 24 hours at a time! Feel empowered as you begin to restore your well-being! There is so much false information online about how to stop being an emotional eater. I am living proof that not only is that not an option, it is unnecessary! The only sustainable option is to "start where you are with what you've got [to retrain your thinking]" as Bob Proctor said so often.

You have the opportunity to use my MTM methodology as your powerful catalyst of real change as you evolve into the person you intend to become, 24 hours at a time, at any age! You can develop your self-esteem, your self-reliance and your self-worth as you use your powerful imagination to see your ideal body when you look in the mirror. This is so much fun! You will gain momentum as your guilt and shame goes away because of your new thoughts, behaviors, and habits. No one needs to know that your inner transformation has begun but your enthusiasm will begin to show. You will be on your way back to mastering the one and only you! Our time on this planet is shorter than we want to admit and the time is now for you to develop into the dignified person you intend to become!

- The state of your life is nothing more than a reflection of your state of mind. -Dr. Wayne Dyer
- Without doubt, the most common weakness of all human beings is the habit of leaving their minds open to the negative influence of other people. -Napoleon Hill

By focusing on decision-making in 5-minute windows, 24 hours at a time, you create your future. Here is a list of some powerful thought leaders who I followed on my inner journey. You may find their teachings helpful as well:

- Bob Proctor and Sandy Gallagher of Proctor Gallagher Institute – Thinking into Results
- David Goggins, ultra-marathoner, author of *Can't Hurt Me* "Go into the deep chambers in your mind to face those demons to develop courage and faith in your ability to do what it takes."
- Dr. Wayne Dyer, spiritual author, eloquent speaker "I am that I say I am."
- Les Brown, thought leader and speaker, "It's possible!"
- Tom Bilyeu, co-founder of Quest and the co-founder and host of Impact Theory, for his valuable insights on mind chemistry and igniting human potential.
- Tony Robbins, NLP master, the one and only.
- Dean Graziosi, worldwide expert on marketing. You can make an impact by sharing your life experiences. Hint: your younger self is your ideal client.
- Dr. Joe Dispenza,
- Choose to be defined by a vision of your future instead of by memories of your past. Act like the person you intend to become! Over time you will draw your future to you, it is inevitable.
- Learn to Think Greater Than You Feel in the present moment.
- Teach your body emotionally what your compelling future will feel like ahead of time, by getting crystal clear on what you really want. You are essentially remembering your future!
- Combine a clear intention with an elevated emotion, lean into the feeling, stay in the uncomfortable feeling of the unknown in the present moment. As you get comfortable with being uncomfortable, you will develop and grow.
- As you get out of your head and into your heart, you will feel whole and heal yourself of the inadequacies and feelings of lack. As a result you will no longer need to look outside of yourself for your self-worth!

I am thrilled for you to have learned my methodology as you embark on your deeply personal journey of transformation! Please understand that it is possible for you to restore your self-esteem as you develop control over your thoughts, behaviors, and actions. As you make better choices in 5-minute windows, 24 hours at a time, you will evolve into a proud role model for yourself, your loved ones, any children, and spouse. You and they deserve you to be at your best, and to lead by example, of what is possible when you think better thoughts about yourself. No need to waste one more moment beating yourself up about the past. You cannot change it! It simply led you to right now.

- Kids don't remember what you try to teach them. They remember what you are. -Jim Henson

You are not stuck! Right now is all you have and all you will ever need to create your future!

READY TO TAKE THE NEXT STEP?

https://linktr.ee/MasterTheMomentInc – to book my time (via Calendly)
I will help you to empower yourself! 1:1 for Emotional Eaters: Your Roadblocks and Desires
Facebook *Profile* @Conni Blanchard
Facebook *Page* @MasterTheMomentInc

ABOUT THE AUTHOR

Conni Blanchard, president of Master The Moment, Inc. was a deeply emotional eater who rewarded and punished herself with food for decades. She transformed herself by learning to master the moment. By retraining her thinking, she dropped 10 sizes and her body went from being her worst enemy to her best friend. As a mentor for Emotional Eaters, a catalyst for real change, she shares her authentic life experience to restore self-worth, a sense of dignity, and hope for women who suffer from poor self-esteem, no self-reliance and debilitating self-talk. She currently lives outside of Boston, MA with her husband. This year they proudly share the milestone of their daughter's college graduation.

https://linktr.ee/MasterTheMomentInc

"You are braver than you
believe, smarter than you seem,
and stronger than you think."

Winnie-the-Pooh (A. A. Milne)

Printed in the United States
by Baker & Taylor Publisher Services